THE THREE STEPS TO MLM SUCCESS

BECOME A SUCCESSFUL MLM ENTREPENEUR

ANNE SCHLOSSER

Copyright © Anne Schlosser
All Rights Reserved.

ISBN 978-1-63920-727-5

This book has been published with all efforts taken to make the material error-free after the consent of the author. However, the author and the publisher do not assume and hereby disclaim any liability to any party for any loss, damage, or disruption caused by errors or omissions, whether such errors or omissions result from negligence, accident, or any other cause.

While every effort has been made to avoid any mistake or omission, this publication is being sold on the condition and understanding that neither the author nor the publishers or printers would be liable in any manner to any person by reason of any mistake or omission in this publication or for any action taken or omitted to be taken or advice rendered or accepted on the basis of this work. For any defect in printing or binding the publishers will be liable only to replace the defective copy by another copy of this work then available.

Contents

1. Previous Work: Authenticity　　　1
2. Step 1: The Motive　　　3
3. Step 2: Awake Interest　　　9
4. Step 3: Keep Them Informed　　　11
5. Conclusion　　　14
6. Epilogue　　　15

Disclaimer　　　17

I
Previous Work: Authenticity

The often underestimated factor in every one of our sponsorins is authenticity. Those that act like an exremely successful young entrepeneur and wish to convince the whole world to be exactly like him, will not be able to help many be like him, if he is not sure himself how to fill his sports car (a lease, obviously). This kind of entrepeneurs show their lack of ability and hardly anyone would wish to join their team, to be their partner or sublet for him.

In my experience, he would have much more success if he were to say: «I am going through a rough patch and I have found something that impressed me both as a product and a business model. I would like to talk to you about it, because I think you could be ineterested.»

Authenticity has something to do with identity, when it comes to business development. New entrepreneurs must be capable of relating the product to the company. If you think your product or company are great, then it will be much easier for you to convice other people of it. Memorizing products, concepts or benefits will not be useful.

If you don´t have a positive attitude regarding the product and the company, you should invest the time to work on this. The more enthusiasm you are capable of showing, the easier it would be for others to pick up that feeling.

II

Step 1: The Motive

Many people taking part into Network Marketing, regardless of the products they offer, are every event´s nightmare. I have experienced this with many members, networks and club meetings. They grasp one person´s attention, and then the other, and they bless these people with their overenthusiastic sales pitch, through which they announce their products and ability to generate «passive income». As the day goes by, they pile up more and more rejecton and their speech is harder to deliver.

Source of Mistakes 1

If you deicide to go for it this way, I will give you a hint that is worth alone a thousand times more than what you paid fort his book: «Listen! With this method, you can only accomplish two things: First, to successfully make everyone, even those interested in your offer run away, in an attempt to protect themselves. And, second, nobody will want to talk to you. Some will even manage to avoid you in future reunions.»

This type of events are a wonderful way to meet new partners and clients, but it must be learned how to successfullly conduct them.

The first step in these kinds of meetings is to establish contact and approach people who still do not know you. Unsuccessful entrepreneurs always surround themselves with the same people they already know and then ask themselves why nothing is changing in their lives. Successful entrepeneurs always look for new people. If you want to spare the stomach ache, I recommend you to follow my advice.

To sumarize, this ist he abridged version: speak to people! These events are, in most cases, wonderful opportunities to meet new people, who will be grateful that you had the courage to take the first step.

Source of Mistakes 2

Now, this ist he moment where many people trip. Once the ice has been broken a little, they start talking to their counterparts about the offer. They try to get the message across by establishing that this ist he right path for said counterpart. Thus, this becomes a threat, because we are implying that a complete strangre has our exact same problem and is motivated by the same wishes we are. You have to understand that because your dream of a passive income of a few thousand euros, it is not the same for everyone, and not everybody will have the exact same ambition.

I, personally have noticed to go into this direction much too early in the conversation. An older man was standing in front of me and I began telling him about my model, implying I knew the best way to complement his pension. I was sure I had the key points to inspire him. Unfortunately, I was wrong, and I realized an hour later, when he was asked to the stage, since he was sponsoring the event, that he was an action holder for a world renowned bank and it hit me that for the duration of an hour I had been trying to convince a billionaire that I could help him complement his pension, by selling food supplements.

Source of Mistakes 3

The third, just a signifivative, mistake happens when you try to carry on with this procedure an build a good conversation to have the oportunity to meet an interesting person and build a good relationship through discussing your business model. Almost nobody goes to this kind of events to buy food supplements, kitchen appliances or insurance. Long story short, you are in the wrong place.

Source of Mistakes 4

In case you don´t know any person who wants to listen to you when you tell your story life, opinions, hopes and dreams, then it is a great idea to attend an appropiate event to meet them. There, you will be able to lower your mental sytress and listen to everybody else. But that is not how you find a new partner or client.

Make your counterpart interested, and find out what he is interested in, what moves him and what are his challenges and successes to that date.

Best case scenario, you will learn about your counterpart and better your autodevelopment. At least, you will get to have a nice conversation. And, as an added value, you will get to leave your counterpath with a positive opinion of yourself.

We all love talking about ourselves, and we try to give an impression of a positive attitude to our counterpart. Anybody who shows interest in us, must be an interesting person. Furthermore, you will have another motive and that is to know why this person could become your new client or partner and receive him, in many cases, on a silver platter.

Source of Mistakes 5

Once you comprehend the «why» of you counterpart, nothing sounds more sensible as using this «weapon» against him to present him the solution to his problems. Many feel tempted to present him with a contract or a pile of requisites. And that is exactly the biggest mistake. From the moment you begin your conversation, you will believe you are able to recognize exactly why this offer you are presenting is perfect for said person. Nevertheless, this person is not ready to grasp all the information and must sit to analyze the subject a bit more and without any rush. In this moment, he is much too busy.

Furthermore, this can stillbe thought of as «mistake number three». You are not here to sell a thing, your goal must be securing the contact details of your counterpart. Nothing else! Make mental notes of the data and key words in your conversation. Discuss a future meeting. But remember: an appointment for your business in *network marketing*, whatever the type, *has no place here*.

Examples of «Why»

New members always ask me once and again which is a promising «why» that can get results. The answer is very simple: There is a different answer for every person. It´s something that both motivates and interests them while capturing their attention and representing opportunities for the future. But, it can also be a reaction based on fear, anger, or even the wish to «show the world I made it». Below, you will find a few examples I will give you the different «why of people», which I have encountered through my career in network marketing:

Miss M is a mother and a homemaker. Her children study during the day and she does not look for a temporary job, in order to be able to spend time with the kids when they are in vacation. A determined and concise career in network marketing ist he best solution for her to have her own income and her children will not experience the absence of her mother at home.

Mister L. is successful within his profession. But now, he has become the oldest person in the company and he wonders whether they will keep him employed until the time for his retirement comes. With network marketing, he would be able to get the extra income needed to keep everything going until the day he retires, (and even further after).

- Mrs. S wants to prove everyone that she is not only an excelent homemaker, but a woman capable of brining home the bread.
- Mrs. W is a widown and she can barely make ends meet. The aditional earnings coming from network marketing make her income whole. Plus, she has the chance to meet many new people.
- Mrs. L has lost over thirty kilograms with the help of food supplements and wants to help other people suffering from obesity.
- Mr. P is a personal trainer who works on comission and has
- liberated himself from the time for money trap, through the construction of his own marketing network. Now, finally, he can afford the luxury to take out a bit more money if he has a sick day or wishes to take a vacation.

His partners and clients in the network marketing are mostly clients of his fitness programm.
- Mrs. W dreamt of taking a vacation in the Caribbean during years. With her normal income coming from event organization, this would never be real. With this aditional passive income, she gets so much money that she goes on the most exotic vacations the world can offer every single year.
- Mrs. G owns a small hairdresser and can barely make ends meet. Since she casually offers beauty products to her clients, not only does she get additional income, but new clients. They recommend the business to their acquaintances, not only to cut and wash their hair, but to solve other problems related to beauty and personal care.

This list does not include every motive there is. Everybody has a different «why» that will make them interested in your offer. Only if you recognize the why of a human being, and not any «why», but the one that actually concerns your potential client, can you move forward to the second step.

III

Step 2: Awake Interest

As it was mentioned before, you can only advance to the second step if you have found your counterpart´s why. If this is not the case, study your target a bit more before meeting him once more. In order to get to know him better in a casual environment and not a business one, drink a beer after work, a cup of coffee or cake, or tag along to an event he is going, etc.

The second step is very simple: If you already know your counterparts «WHY», call to arrange a meeting a few days later. It is very important that you don´t make this call to soon. You don´t want to come off as someone who just wants to get to sponsor him. The call cannot be made too late either, because it is important that the memory of your positive attitude remains fresh on your counterpart´s mind.

This call could go something like: «We had a very interesting conversation the other day,... you told me that,... I could not forget about it and I believe I can offer you a solution,... How about we meet up and discuss it? Maybe that is the answer you have been looking for».

Source of Mistakes 6

Even when we reach the point of making the call, we can make mistakes. First, your counterpart will ask if it´s possible to know what your offer is about. Avoid giving him information over the phone, even though that might not be simple. One of the things that has worked for me is telling them that I cannot tell them over the phone because I would like to make sure I understood their needs correctly. In other cases, we could also say it would be better to show them the solution on the spot, and even when it sounds illogical, we could say it would make us very happy to see them again and further discuss our the previous conversation. Remember: pression creates a reaction and it will almost always cost you potential clients.

Source of Mistakes 7

The second mistake commonly made in this situation, is to assure you have the solution. Once you make this assumption, you deprive your counterpart of the chance to evaluate this. But if the «solution» promised does not live up to your counterpart´s expectations, the risk of rejection is too high. This is totally unnecessary.

Build your whole argument as a question, in the sense of: «I could have a possible solution, let´s see what you think of it.» The goal is not to make your counterpart feel like you are trying to sell him something, but rather that you are looking for a solution together. He will surely begin accepting your invitations to speak in the future if he notices he can say no, without that being a problem for you or your relationship.

It is sensible not to leave an open date fort he meeting. Offer a couple of dates in which you have time so your counterpart can choose and a possible convenient

IV
Step 3: Keep Them Informed

Now you have managed to complete the two first steps with success and even when your time is money, literally, be careful not to keep creating pressure, neither for you, ort he other parts. Pression generates rush reactions, and you don´t want that.

Source of Mistakes 8

Join the conversation, but not as a salesman. Power Point presentations, flyers and everything else can stay at home. You only agreed to discuss an idea you have. It´s not the moment to push a contract in any one´s ace. I, in my experiecne, have noticed that in these discussions there is normally nothing more than a big block and two different colored pins.

Keep talking freely. You are not here to be judged or to get a degree, but to consider an idea together which you are going to show, because it is interesting and you are trying to answer the «why» your counterpart has. Present your idea on paper, but remember, a poor drawn sketch is much better than a professionaly printed four ink flyer.

Make your counterpart´s interest grow little by little, even when this means arranging another meeting to close the deal. Some salesman arrive at this appointment with all materials in hand. I try to leave this for further appointments, thus not giving my counterpart the idea that I am trying to manipulate him. But everyone must discover what works better for him and their clients.

Source of Mistakes 9

There is still people living under the motto: No, means you still need more information. This makes no sense at all. People have every right not to take a step at any moment. You must accept that and let your counterpart know. Those who create pressure in a situation and then try to soften it with arguments lose all the advantages.

Your counterpart, at this point, has already listened to you and has enough information in order for his decision to be respected. We can definitely store this person in a «not yet ready» archive or keep in touch. That does not mean we should follow him day and night, but rather that we should keep informing them of interesting subjects, but not promoting our business to them. It would be much better to send him information that interests him, share news with them when we run into them or invite them to an event from our MLM company. In this business we call this «water», which we can then spread over this tiny plant that will eventually grow.

My previous experience shows that sooner or later (this could sometimes take up to a year) I can lead a great amount of people to a successful conclusion, because I understand the real why. Even some people, who sensed my positive attitude and liked the way I treated them, recommend me to people, before they covince themselves. They are completely sure that I will keep my positive energy and value those around me.

V

Conclusion

You have reached your final goal. This is the moment for the last interview, Ideally, you would have answered all of your counterparts questions and it is important you make it official by putting it into a contract.

Nevertheless, mistakes can still be made. Many salesmen fear that their counterparts will say no and do not ask the final question. Talk to your counterpart, while he signs up[3] to this enterprise or he agrees to buying products. Ideally, you would fill this application together.

If your counterpart signs, you are the winner. If he does not, ask what was missing to convince him of signing. You may get an immeadiate answer, and if that was not the case, you will have a reason to ask later.

Unless the subject «closing the deal» makes you sick to your stomach, every advice I have shared with you will be very useful.

[3]Depending on the adequate option fort he member, the pertinent option will be chosen: Society Contract, Franchise Sale, Purchase Order...

VI
Epilogue

Dear reader,

You have studied and practiced the three steps to sell and you are already acquainted with the most common mistakes. This is the time to put what you learn into action. You will realize that maybe not anything will work at first. Take the time to learn and better your personal techinique. In the end, you will not only mae your network grow, but you will meet a lot of interesting people.

The subtitle of this book is Become A Successful MLM Entrepeneur. I am aware this is a rather ambitious objective and of course you will not manage to convince one hundred percent of your clients. If we were looking after that kind of results, we would have to try it in other fields, like esotherism, but certainly not in the field of MLM.

What I can tell you, even when it is not a promise, is that the success you have recruiting new members will increase considerably by following these steps. An increase of 1:30 to 1:3 is enormous. Furthermore, it reduces and makes the procedure much more precise to those who are afraid to get a no for answer.

I wish you have fun, meet many interesting people and have a successful business!

Yours, Anne Schlosser

PS: It would make me very happy if I could get your feedback on this book. It would give me an opportunity to optimize my method to maintain success.

Disclaimer

Introduction

By using this book, you accept this disclaimer in full.

No advice

The book contains information. The information is not advice and should not be treated as such.

No representations or warranties

To the maximum extent permitted by applicable law and subject to section below, we exclude all representations, warranties, undertakings and guarantees relating to the book.

Without prejudice to the generality of the foregoing paragraph, we do not represent, warrant, undertake or guarantee:

- that the information in the book is correct, accurate, complete or non-misleading.

- that the use of the guidance in the book will lead to any particular outcome or result.

Limitations and exclusions of liability

The limitations and exclusions of liability set out in this section and elsewhere in this disclaimer: are subject to section 6 below; and govern all liabilities arising under the disclaimer or in relation to the book, including liabilities arising in contract, in tort (including negligence) and for breach of statutory duty.

We will not be liable to you in respect of any losses arising out of any event or events beyond our reasonable control.

DISCLAIMER

We will not be liable to you in respect of any business losses, including without limitation loss of or damage to profits, income, revenue, use, production, anticipated savings, business, contracts, commercial opportunities or goodwill.

We will not be liable to you in respect of any loss or corruption of any data, database or software.

We will not be liable to you in respect of any special, indirect or consequential loss or damage.

Exceptions

Nothing in this disclaimer shall: limit or exclude our liability for death or personal injury resulting from negligence; limit or exclude our liability for fraud or fraudulent misrepresentation; limit any of our liabilities in any way that is not permitted under applicable law; or exclude any of our liabilities that may not be excluded under applicable law.

Severability

If a section of this disclaimer is determined by any court or other competent authority to be unlawful and/or unenforceable, the other sections of this disclaimer continue in effect.

If any unlawful and/or unenforceable section would be lawful or enforceable if part of it were deleted, that part will be deemed to be deleted, and the rest of the section will continue in effect.

Law and jurisdiction

This disclaimer will be governed by and construed in accordance with Swiss law, and any disputes relating to this disclaimer will be subject to the exclusive jurisdiction of the courts of Switzerland.

www.ingramcontent.com/pod-product-compliance
Lightning Source LLC
Chambersburg PA
CBHW020716180526
45163CB00008B/3118